National Landscape Conservation System
BLM Colorado Implementation Strategy
2013

BLM

COLORADO

Executive Summary

Colorado's National Conservation Lands encompass approximately one million acres:

- 3 national conservation areas (Dominguez-Escalante, Gunnison Gorge, McInnis Canyons)
- 5 wilderness areas (Black Ridge Canyons, Dominguez Canyon, Gunnison Gorge, Powderhorn, Uncompahgre)
- 1 national historic trail (Old Spanish)
- 1 national scenic trail (Continental Divide)
- 1 national monument (Canyons of the Ancients)
- 54 wilderness study areas

Colorado public lands inspire and challenge humanity through a broad spectrum of landscapes and opportunities. From 800-year old Ancestral Puebloan settlements situated in present day Canyons of the Ancients National Monument and industry and settlement support showcased on trade routes like the Old Spanish Trail, to today's busy hives of recreation in places like McInnis Canyon and Gunnison Gorge national conservation areas, our landscapes have embodied a vision of the possible. Colorado's residents recognize the value in our many diverse resources, ensuring these places retain their qualities for future generations while they serve us today. The National Landscapes Conservation System (National Conservation Lands) consists of presidential and congressionally-designated lands managed by the Bureau of Land Management as legacies to America's natural and cultural heritage. In Colorado, one-eighth of the agency's surface responsibilities have this special status, which were primarily designated through local community initiatives.

The National Conservation Lands mission is to conserve, protect, and restore these nationally significant landscapes recognized for their outstanding cultural, ecological, and scientific values. In 2007, BLM Colorado worked with partners to create a statewide National Landscape Conservation System Strategic Plan, which focused primarily on the national monument and national conservation areas. The plan (available online) provided BLM Colorado with direction and management benchmarks. Now, five years later, following the transition of the management system to law, the BLM crafted a National Landscape Conservation System 15-year Strategy. This guidance is continued through the BLM's 2012 policy manuals for National Monuments, National Conservation Areas, Wilderness, Wilderness Study Areas, National Scenic and Historic Trails, and Wild and Scenic Rivers.

The time is right to reflect on the 2007 Colorado plan through the lens of the national strategy to ensure its relevance. This new document reflects the efforts of all of Colorado's field offices in coordination with our partners and our three Resource Advisory Committees. The Colorado implementation plan accommodates fluctuations in management resources and the needs of diverse landscapes. This plan will serve, to support the direction of our National Conservation Lands program at the state and local level for the next five years, and encourages communities to recognize opportunities for shared stewardship. This executive summary, like the implementation strategy, mirrors the national strategy document, but with ground level applications.

Throughout the plan "objects and values" are prioritized in management decisions. This language references the defining resources of the area that are called out for conservation, protection and restoration in the designating language for each National Conservation Land. For National Scenic and Historic Trails, the defining resources are referred to as "purpose and need"; for Wild and Scenic Rivers, "outstandingly remarkable values"; and for wilderness and WSAs, "wilderness characteristics". In this document those special resources for all areas are referenced as "objects and values". Designating language also identifies the manner in which grandfathered uses are protected, a characteristic of National Conservation Lands that reinforces local stewardship and brings ties us to our history.

The four theme summaries below mirror the national strategy over the next five years to provide catalysts for innovation and stewardship. The existing Colorado Strategy maps the route to address National Conservation Lands goals. The summary reflects the overarching systems that are tied to local nuances within the larger Implementation Strategy.

Theme 1: Ensuring the Conservation, Protection, and Restoration of National Landscape Conservation System (National Conservation Lands) Values

State Strategic Approach: Prioritize maintaining the healthy, wild, and open character of National Conservation Lands, guided by the purposes for which the landscapes were designated.

- Tier all actions through the hierarchical order from designation, resource management plan, science plan, and special stipulations to proceed with transparent commitments to on-the-ground actions.
- Tie landscape research to community partnerships, supporting inquiry-focused institutions and stewardship-oriented organizations' involvement in the ongoing generation of data for scientific decision-making.
- Ensure outreach and interpretation convey the balance of science within the multiple use mandate.

- Clearly define similarities and differences in the management of Wilderness and Wilderness Study Areas. Guide management of wilderness characteristics through monitoring, application of the Minimum Requirements Decision Guide, and the Keeping It Wild Interagency Strategy.
- Limit discretionary uses to those compatible with the conservation, protection, and restoration of the values for which National Conservation Lands were designated

Theme 2: Collaboratively Managing the National Conservation Lands as Part of the Larger Landscape

State Strategic Approach: Establish management strategies that reflect protecting, conserving, and restoring significant resource values of National Conservation Lands within regional landscape ecosystems. Build stewardship among stakeholders across boundaries.

- Reflect management of National Conservation Lands as a part of the surrounding landscapes considering the socioeconomic goals of the community through planning.
- Participate in external planning efforts to preserve sustainable economic interests, protect and restore migratory corridors, and integrate climate change models and fire prevention adaptive management.
- Underscore the opportunities and benefits of partnering with educational institutions and streamline processes that promote collaboration.
- Support sustainable, high quality recreation experiences and quality of life outcomes for local communities and user groups through BLM Colorado's Recreation Strategy.

Theme 3: Raising Awareness of the Value and Benefits of the BLM's National Conservation Lands

State Strategic Approach: Promote safe and appropriate public access and foster visitor enjoyment, appreciation, and learning opportunities to provide for enriching and inspiring experiences. Improve internal and external information sharing and enhance the awareness and identity of the National Conservation Lands in Colorado.

- Consistently present facets of the BLM multiple use mandate and the significance of the National Conservation Lands through external communications.
- Ensure education and interpretation are part of recreation planning, communication of land health issues and protection strategies, and building youth participation in conservation practices.
- Explore opportunities to promote diverse participation, which is integral to outreach programs, recreation, and collaborative projects.
- Expand infrastructure to support volunteers and partners to further accomplishments through expanded stewardship.

Theme 4: Building on the BLM's Commitment to Conservation

State Strategic Approach: Commit to conserving, protecting, and restoring special values within Colorado's National Conservation Lands. Prioritize maintaining the healthy, wild, and open character of the landscapes. Provide sustainable funding and staffing necessary to appropriately manage National Conservation Lands in Colorado.

- Promote awareness that all resource disciplines are integral to addressing the scope of responsibilities associated with each area, recognizing best practices and publishing accomplishments such as research project conclusions and managers reports.
- Recognize and promote the National Landscape Conservation System's mission as an integral part of the broader BLM mission.
- Update internal mechanisms such as budget planning, intranet sites, and cadastral data to support multiple engagement and contribution to adaptive management.
- Efficiently use internal funding opportunities such as deferred maintenance and reimbursable accounts while exploring partnership opportunities to build capacity and accomplish stewardship projects.

Theme 1: Ensuring the Conservation, Protection, and Restoration of National Landscape Conservation System (National Conservation Lands) Values

National Emphasis:
- Policy Development
- Science
- Data Management

State Strategic Approach:
Prioritize maintaining the healthy, wild, and open character of National Conservation Lands, guided by the purposes for which the landscapes were designated.

1A: Prioritize efforts that demonstrate conservation, protection, and restoration, and illustrate their connection to BLM Strategic Goals for Resource Use and Protection.

State Level Actions:

- Work across program boundaries within the agency to highlight the breadth of resources conserved through the National Conservation Lands.
- Support cross-program dialogue with resource specialists to promote understanding of planning processes specific to National Conservation Lands.
- Ensure statewide outreach carries the messaging of similarities and differences in management requirements for National Conservation Lands.
- Promote understanding and integration of National Conservation Lands policy manuals through trainings and webinars for state, district, and field offices (completed by all program staff by 2015).

Unit Level Actions:

- Underscore enabling legislation, objects, and values in Resource Management Plans (RMP), activity plans, business plans, and science plans.
- Ensure RMP decisions and implementation actions reinforce the conservation mission of the National Landscape Conservation System.
- Frame initiatives within the context of prioritizing objects and values; respond to resource changes with adaptive management.
- Develop special stipulations to address region-specific needs (e.g., natural, cultural, recreational, etc.).

1B: Foster and promote scientific research within the National Conservation Lands.

State Level Actions:

- Develop geospatial data layers and maps for key resources in easy-to-interpret formats to facilitate unit-level assessments, decision making, and internal and external information sharing.
- Develop guidelines for research in wilderness and wilderness study areas (WSA) by 2015.
- Facilitate generating protocols for professional-quality data collection through citizen science projects.
- Establish partnerships with research-focused organizations to support local research efforts through Memoranda of Understanding (MOU).
- Incorporate monitoring in base workloads.
- Develop a funding strategy to support research requirements.
- Share research findings in the BLM daily report, E-News, and other media outlets.

Unit Level Actions:

- Maintain interdisciplinary team involvement in the management of each unit to ensure a full mix of resource management appropriate for the area.
- Develop and implement comprehensive weed-management programs for each unit.
- Implement BLM Assessment, Inventory, and Monitoring Strategy (http://www.blm.gov/style/medialib/blm/wo/Information_Resources_Management/policy/ib_attachments/2012.Par.53766.File.dat/IB2012-080_att1.pdf).

- Complete landscape health assessments and improve landscape health within units by incorporating landscape health objectives into RMPs and activities.

1C: Establish better understanding for scientific decision-making regarding managing landscapes and significant resource values for conservation, protection, and restoration.

State Level Actions:

- Develop a WSA monitoring strategy (implemented by 2015). This should include a comparison of current WSA conditions to originally inventoried WSA conditions to determine restoration priorities.
- Link field and district office actions to national strategies in discussions and outreach efforts.
- Develop a program overview for science study areas.
- Create a toolkit for environmental education and interpretation programs.
- Identify and address resource and funding needs to implement the science strategy.
- Expedite processes for partnership MOUs, assistance agreements, and contracting.
- Foster a statewide culture encouraging academic involvement.
- Create and promote opportunities for traditional science research.

Unit Level Actions:

- Work with the state office to set annual targets to complete inventories of the natural and cultural resources, objects, and values for which national monuments, national conservation areas (NCA) were established.
- Tier research activities from baseline data and integrate climate change models.
- Promote local awareness for ties between management actions and unit science plans.
- Develop partnerships, collaborative projects, and activities that result in specific conservation and restoration benefits.
- Develop and tie on-the-ground laboratories (learning landscapes, living classrooms, etc.) and science study areas to regional environmental education initiatives.
- Promote agency awareness of opportunities to use the National Conservation Lands as focused research locations.
- Use interpretation to reveal the National Conservation Lands' relationship to the BLM's multiple use mission.

1D: Build a scientific foundation with adaptive management strategies for decision-making processes.

State Level Actions:

- Identify and pursue key partnerships to support a comprehensive scientific knowledge base.
- Identify research (accomplished or underway) relevant to the National Conservation Lands, promote awareness, and support unit landscape science goals.

Unit Level Actions:

- Designate a collateral duty science coordinator for each NCA and national monument. This person will serve as the contact for science providers submitting research requests through the BLM Science Web Portal.
- Develop unit-specific science plans that identify and guide the unit's scientific goals and efforts.
- Conduct comprehensive, cost-effective inventory and monitoring programs to identify ecosystems, unique values, and sensitive areas, and to track trends and changes in resource condition.
- Identify and address gaps in the data needed to support land-use plan implementation priorities; these gaps can serve as a basis for soliciting science providers and funding, as well as a way to highlight accomplishments.
- Share science plans, methods, and results internally and externally.
- Complete grazing allotment monitoring, compliance, and evaluations, and implement actions to meet land health objectives.
- Acquire and coordinate baseline ecological information for the National Conservation Lands and surrounding landscapes.

1E: Limit discretionary uses to those compatible with the conservation, protection, and restoration of the values for which National Conservation Lands were designated.

State Level Actions:

- Ensure multiple uses are consistent with protections afforded to each specific National Conservation Land in applicable laws and relevant designations through planning.

- Provide support, guidance, and outreach materials for complex issues such as valid existing rights for mining, grazing, and the application of the Minimum Requirement Decision Guide for wilderness.
- Support the interdisciplinary planning process to develop appropriate travel networks and recreation opportunities that reflect the conservation, protection and enhancement of the resources the area was established to protect.
- Promote clarity about the policy and management differences between wilderness and WSAs.
- Conduct outreach to illustrate conservation's role in multiple use management on National Conservation Lands.

Unit Level Actions:

- Limit discretionary uses to those compatible with conservation, protection, and restoration of the values for which National Conservation Lands were designated.
- Work with holders of valid existing rights to balance uses with National Conservation Lands resources and values.
- Recognize or create opportunities for incompatible uses in regions surrounding the National Conservation Lands.
- Restore unauthorized areas through travel management.
- Improve visitor outreach with site-specific information, interactions with agency personnel, partners, and resource patrols to improve voluntary compliance with rules and regulations and reduce illegal activities.
- Employ the use of non-law-enforcement personnel to help achieve regulatory compliance and resource protection.
- Remove federally-owned facilities and structures that are identified as unnecessary and do not possess cultural or historic significance.

National Emphasis:
- Ecosystem-based Management
- Conservation Values in Planning
- Communicating Collaboration Success Stories

State Strategic Approach:
Establish management strategies that reflect protecting, conserving, and restoring significant resource values of the National Conservation Lands within regional landscape ecosystems. Build stewardship among stakeholders across boundaries.

2A: Emphasize an ecosystem-based approach to manage National Conservation Lands in the context of the surrounding landscape.

State Level Actions:
- Use large-scale assessments, such as the Colorado Plateau Rapid Ecoregional Assessment and wilderness characteristics inventories, to identify how National Conservation Lands fit within the broader landscape and work with partners to apply available science in managing public lands at the landscape-scale.
- Establish MOUs with land management agencies and adjacent landowners to work together on landscape and development planning.
- Promote public awareness to encourage landscape-level thinking and stewardship.
- Offer a clearinghouse of research projects and initiatives focused on large landscape research.

Theme 2: Collaboratively Managing the National Conservation Lands as Part of the Larger Landscape

11

- Map large-scale ecological corridors within landscapes to identify key linkages to maintain or increase habitat connectivity and provide for sustainable populations of native species.

Unit Level Actions:

- Emphasize restoration and protection of native species within their historic ranges.
- In areas of National Conservation Lands designated for their cultural significance, manage cultural resources within the larger context of the landscape and adjoining lands.
- Follow the BLM's policies to implement the U.S. Fish and Wildlife Service's threatened and endangered species biological conservation requirements.
- Work collaboratively across boundaries through planning to preserve migratory corridors.
- Integrate climate change models as they are developed and fire management strategies into plans, as appropriate.
- Participate in vulnerability assessments for critical resources at risk from direct and indirect impacts of climate change.

2B: Adopt a cross-jurisdictional, community-based approach to landscape-level conservation planning and management. Identify and protect lands that are critical to the long-term ecological sustainability of the landscape.

State Level Actions:

- Work with the Southern Rockies Landscape Conservation Cooperative and Regional Climate Centers to coordinate planning and managing National Conservation Lands at a landscape-scale (http://www.doi.gov/lcc/Southern-Rockies.cfm).
- Facilitate information and data sharing on landscape-level resource planning and management with federal and state agencies, state and local governments, and tribes.
- Support site-specific partnering efforts to build community collaboration.
- Use the BLM Science Web Portal to inform science providers of research opportunities, track activities, and monitor research work to ensure it complies with laws, regulations, and land-use planning decisions.
- Support collaborative planning with networked internal and external databases.
- Promote accomplishment and circulation of socioeconomic studies to augment planning resources.

Unit Level Actions:

- Build and sustain relationships with local communities and user groups to foster cooperative conservation and community stewardship.
- Develop and maintain cooperative agreements with gateway communities, stewardship groups, educational institutions, industry, and friends groups to accomplish priority on-the-ground work, and address key issues such as biodiversity, connectivity and climate change.
- Work with the public and partners to identify potential inholdings for incorporation within National Conservation Lands unit boundaries, giving higher priority to lands that enhance ecological connectivity or protect nationally significant landscapes that have outstanding cultural, ecological, and scientific values.
- Build employee skills and redefine priority workloads to integrate community partnerships within day-to-day business to build stewardship capacity.
- Support community science and traditional science initiatives.
- Partner with local libraries to promote natural and cultural resource awareness.
- Prioritize partnerships, collaborative projects, and activities that result in conservation and restoration benefits.
- Provide, support, and mentor local leadership in conservation and preservation practices.
- Establish partnerships with outside governmental agency law enforcement through formal agreements to support public education and enforcement presence.
- Leverage funds through place-based partnerships to use external resources and revenue streams, as well as volunteer resources.

2C: Develop and initiate outreach programs in partnership with educational institutions to accomplish research and applied science, as well as communicate needs and successes.

State Level Actions:

- Tie statewide initiatives to higher education networks and extensions; build relationships, cooperate, and collaborate with educational institutions in outreach efforts.
- Broaden public awareness of the National Conservation Lands through existing national, state and local partnerships.
- Establish overarching MOUs with conservation organizations to support field office relationships with chapters.

Unit Level Actions:

- Engage academia in developing Best Management Practices and restoration projects. Partner on cooperative research funding.
- Assist and support local education institutions in designing and developing curriculum.
- Seek opportunities to partner with regional and international institutions researching similar issues.
- Use science plans as catalysts for landscape-level discussions.
- Share "Keeping it Wild" methodologies with interested private landowners and other land management entities (http://www.wilderness.net/index.cfm?fuse=toolboxes&sec=WC).

2D: Implement Colorado's Recreation Strategy objectives to ensure sustainable high-quality recreation experiences and quality of life outcomes for individuals, communities, economies, and the environment.

State Level Actions:

- Offer a full spectrum of National Conservation Lands opportunities through web outreach.
- Use symbol standards in mapping.
- Use BLM's National Conservation Lands watermark for all National Conservation Lands outreach materials.
- Link the National Conservation Lands science program activities to education, interpretive activities, outreach efforts, and national BLM projects.

- Promote awareness of wilderness and WSAs.
- Establish and maintain a clearinghouse of current education and interpretation products.
- Build capacity for international travelers through targeted messaging and accessible graphics.

Unit Level Actions:

- Develop, maintain, and nurture sustainable travel and tourism partnerships with gateway communities to ensure accurate and beneficial marketing of National Conservation Lands recreation opportunities.
- Consider opportunities for self-exploration, solitude, mechanized and motorized travel through travel management planning.
- Manage motorized areas to minimally impact soils and ecosystems that have the potential to affect resources within National Conservation Lands, in line with BLM policy.
- Support partners' stewardship efforts as appropriate. Make BLM exhibits available to local visitor centers and museums, and share opportunities for interpretation and outreach.
- Train docents and visitor assistants on providing user information for National Conservation Lands.
- Improve and maintain signing, mapping, travel information, and education for National Conservation Lands visitors.
- Generate a website for every unit by 2015.
- Promote family-friendly recreation opportunities.
- Improve and prioritize on-the-ground maintenance programs in coordination with BLM engineering staff.
- Ensure critical public drinking water and sewer systems meet public health standards.
- Provide safety awareness, risk management, and hazard training for employees and volunteers with field public contact responsibilities.
- Use visitor messaging to promote personal responsibility and stewardship for cultural resources.
- Establish a monitoring strategy to detect illegal activities.
- Establish action plans to reduce or eliminate inappropriate activity.

Theme 3: Raising Awareness of the Value and Benefits of the BLM's National Conservation Lands

National Emphasis:
- Communication and Outreach
- Develop Program Strategies
- Engage and Employ Veterans
- Engage and Employ Youth

State Strategic Approach:

Promote safe and appropriate public access. Foster visitor enjoyment, appreciation, and learning opportunities to provide for enriching and inspiring experiences. Improve internal and external information sharing and enhance the awareness and identity of National Conservation Lands throughout Colorado.

3A: Create a strong and consistent identity for National Conservation Lands through signage, information, and outreach initiatives.

State Level Actions:

- Coordinate National Conservation Lands websites, brochures, maps, and other recreation information to ensure consistency in messages, appearance, and content.
- Coordinate program information dissemination between the state, district and field offices.
- Include youth on the production team for outreach materials.
- Create a Colorado National Conservation Lands web page that provides news and updates on issues and accomplishments.

- Build a web-based visual and audio library of National Conservation Lands resources.
- Contribute to the BLM Colorado monthly newsletter to highlight success stories and share research accomplishments with the public.
- In conjunction with the field, identify and highlight specific and distinct recreational opportunities, experiences, and benefits for each unit in Colorado.
- Update and implement an external communications plan, including media outreach packets, to facilitate networking among national, regional, state, and local interest groups.
- Develop and implement a wilderness interpretive plan in coordination with other agencies and partners.
- Develop a Colorado National Landscape Conservation System communications toolkit (brochure, fact sheets, postcards, posters, videos, etc.) that represents all units and highlights the unique characteristics of each area.
- Circulate economic impact and community health studies that document local, regional, and national benefits of National Conservation Lands.
- Continue supporting special outreach projects, as well as major state and national initiatives, such as National Public Lands Day, National Trails Day, etc.
- Develop a Colorado National Conservation Lands traveling exhibit, highlighting science, accomplishments, and partnerships.
- Incorporate BLM guidelines for Quality Built Environments in all units.
- Use current technology, including social networking.

Unit Level Actions:

- Develop and conduct education field trips to National Conservation Lands.
- Complete an annual report to highlight success stories and share monitoring information with the public.
- Make annual reports widely available on BLM Websites.
- Continue working with Take It Outside partners, friends groups, and other partner to build an informed constituency.
- Work with the local Chambers of Commerce, Visitor and Convention Bureaus, and other tourism providers to create links between their web pages and unit web pages.

3B: Communicate that public involvement is critical to ensuring resources exist for future generations.

State Level Actions:

- Strengthen and celebrate existing relationships with volunteers and partners.
- Build capacity for field office volunteer and partnering initiatives at the state level with funding and administrative support.
- Sponsor local grants and agreements training for field and district offices and partners.

Unit Level Actions:

- Develop partnerships, collaborative projects, and activities to achieve specific conservation and restoration benefits; build on existing partner program successes.
- Increase family-focused nature experiences and recreation opportunities.
- Expand services to international travelers and non-English speaking audiences.

3C: Increase capacity for managing volunteers, partners, and relationships by increasing skills internally and using skills available in the community.

State Level Actions:

- Create a toolbox with standard assistance agreements, MOUs, and other required documents to for field offices to use with partnerships.
- Build field office capacity with education opportunities.

Unit Level Actions:

- Designate a collateral duty National Conservation Lands volunteer coordinator in each field office.
- Engage the State Office in planning to streamline the agreements process.
- Dedicate resources to employee skill-building.

3D: Communicate landscape health issues, special values, and protection strategies, and showcase management within National Conservation Lands.

State Level Actions:

- Develop interpretive plans and outreach materials with all National Conservation Lands managers to highlight each area's unique cultural, paleontological, historical, geological, and natural resources.
- Establish a network for relevant education and interpretation products and programs for Colorado's units, supporting outdoor ethics and stewardship.
- Manage a coordinated outreach strategy through collaboration with the field.
- Develop and implement a statewide Junior Explorer Program (http://www.blm.gov/wo/st/en/res/Education_in_BLM/Learning_Landscapes.html).

Unit Level Actions:

- Promote awareness for the objects and values of each unit, as well as the grandfathered rights, creating channels for partners to share the BLM's conservation message.
- Expand Hands on the Land programs with one site tied to each national monument or NCA.
- Incorporate *Leave No Trace* (http://lnt.org/), *Tread Lightly!* (http://treadlightly.org/), *Stay The Trail* (http://staythetrail.org/), and other outdoor ethics curricula into unit interpretive plans.
- Develop interpretive plans and outreach materials specific to each unit, incorporating science and research project information.

- Increase volunteer support and community stewardship by diversifying opportunities and creating innovative partnerships with stakeholders.
- Address the significance of cultural resources in context with the designation of the area through interpretation.
- Build capacity for sustainable travel/tourism partnerships with gateway communities to ensure accurate and beneficial marketing of recreation opportunities.

3E: Promote opportunities for youth stewardship and employment.

State Level Actions:

- Develop and fund opportunities for youth engagement and increase youth recruitment for seasonal and full-time employment opportunities with the National Landscape Conservation System.
- Identify opportunities to meet unit staffing needs through academic internships.
- Develop and expand cooperative agreements with colleges and universities.
- Target partnerships with tribes to preserve traditional science practices.
- Facilitate awareness of national Conservation Lands to reach new audiences.

Unit Level Actions:

- Provide outstanding recreational settings and opportunities for visitors and residents that allow them to explore, learn about, appreciate, feel connected to, and derive targeted physical and social benefits and desired outcomes from these special areas.
- Model and highlight positive outcomes through management practices.
- Include career messages in education and interpretation outreach.

Theme 4: Building on BLM's Commitment to Conservation

National Emphasis:
- Communicate Internally
- Coordinate Policy Across BLM
- Implement National and State National Landscape Conservation System Strategies
- Coordinate Budget

State Strategic Approach:
Commit to conserving, protecting, and restoring special values within National Conservation Lands. Prioritize maintaining the healthy, wild, and open character of the landscapes and provide sustainable funding and staffing necessary for appropriate management.

4A: Develop an internal Colorado communication plan to enhance information sharing within the BLM (nationally and statewide) and emphasize the system's' potential to enhance the BLM as a whole.

State Level Actions:

- Reinforce objects and values for which units have been designated in messaging.
- Develop and provide training to explain National Conservation Lands policy and guidance to aid in the development of land-use plans.

Unit Level Actions:

- Work collaboratively with field office permanent and seasonal staff on special projects, events, field trips, and other outreach efforts.
- Build ownership for units throughout field offices with special event days on National Conservation Lands for BLM employees and families.

4B: Cultivate shared responsibility for the National Conservation Lands conservation mandate as an integral part of BLM's multiple-use, sustained-yield mission.

State Level Actions:

- Provide public affairs support with outreach to educate the public, key decision makers, and the media about Colorado units as part of BLM's multiple use mission.
- Ensure that law enforcement monitoring and enforcement activities place high emphasis on protecting each unit's special resources.

Unit Level Actions:

- Highlight conservation within the context of the multiple use mandate in interpretive exhibits and outreach publications.
- Continue to manage compatible uses and valid existing rights consistent in balance with the values for which each area was designated.
- Engage friends groups and other stakeholders through cooperative agreements extending ownership for the National Conservation Lands mission.

4C: Manage National Conservation Lands as directed by legislation and proclamation.

State Level Actions:

- Post the legislation and proclamation on the unit's website.
- Reinforce ties to other relevant resource specialists and programs.
- Continue sharing staff specialists with field offices and explore new ways to jointly fund other necessary positions between units.
- Implement and showcase examples of best management practices, cooperative conservation, and restoration projects that have wider landscape-level applicability and demonstrate accomplishment of strategic performance goals.
- Promote employee and partner awareness opportunities to extend understanding of resource values.

Unit Level Actions:

- Identify adequate core staff needs, specialist support, skill mix, and base operating costs necessary to meet our legal mandates, achieve "high level" standards, and implement RMPs, wilderness plans, etc.
- Develop comprehensive recreation visitation, economic impact measurements, and monitoring and reporting program(s) applicable to all units.
- Identify program-related targets on employee performance evaluations.

4D: Define high standards of management in cultural, natural, wilderness, recreation, and paleontological resource stewardship, protection, and restoration as well as how these standards can be met by coordinating budgets with other BLM programs.

State Level Actions:

- Develop a shared funding priority plan.
- Standardize methods for measuring, tracking and reporting National Conservation Lands accomplishments.
- Seek partnerships with regional, national, and international scale interest groups; streamline the agreements process.
- Explore opportunities to fund site maintenance and increase visitor services under Federal Lands Recreation Enhancement Act and other national initiatives and programs.

Unit Level Actions:

- Strive for adequate across-the-board funding to support interdisciplinary management.
- Develop and enhance partnerships with friends groups and cooperating associations to build capacity to accomplish ground-level actions.
- Maintain interdisciplinary team involvement in managing each unit to ensure a full mix of resource management as appropriate for the area.
- Continue and expand opportunities for partnerships with friends groups, counties, tourism groups, and other BLM programs.

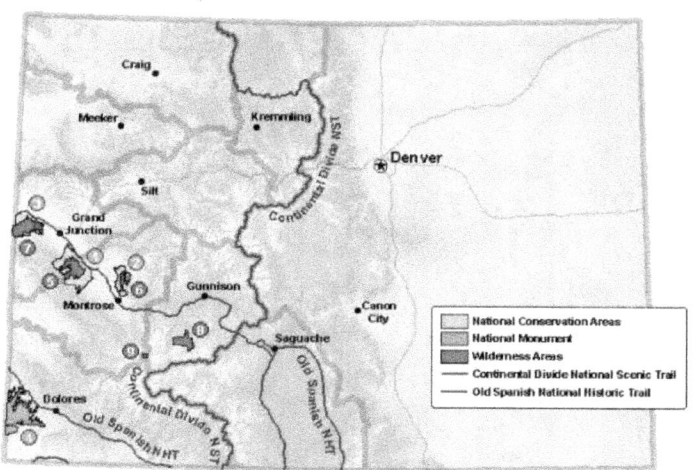

Colorado's National Conservation Lands encompass approximately one million acres:

*   3 national conservation areas (Dominguez-Escalante, Gunnison Gorge, McInnis Canyons)
*   5 wilderness areas (Black Ridge Canyons, Dominguez Canyon, Gunnison Gorge, Powderhorn, Uncompahgre)
*   1 national historic trail (Old Spanish)
*   1 national scenic trail (Continental Divide)
*   1 national monument (Canyons of the Ancients)
*   54 wilderness study areas

For more information visit http://www.blm.gov/co/st/en/BLM_Programs/national_landscape.html or call 303-239-3600.